WALTHAMSTOW

VILLAGE

Published and printed by Walthamstow Historical Society
Vestry House Museum, Vestry Road, London E17 9NH
Monograph New Series No. 38
ISBN(10)   0 85480 061 1
ISBN(13)   978-085480061-2

Text by A.D. Law A.M.A. Revised by Philip C. Plummer.
Maps by W.G.S. Tonkin (Revised).

Cover Illustrations :
Front: Walthamstow Village from the Common, 1820, by Browne,
*   courtesy Vestry House Museum.*
Back: Aerial photograph of Walthamstow Village by
*   Commission Air, courtesy Guy Osborne,*
*   Conservation Officer, L.B.W.F. Enviromental Services.*

Photographs and sketches individually acknowledged
or taken by Roy Ellingham.

Processing and printing : Roy Ellingham.

WALTHAMSTOW VILLAGE

An Account of Church End - the historic centre of Walthamstow

"To stand by the Green at Church End today, with the Vestry House, the Squires' Almshouses, and the old National School meeting ones' view, with the ancient Parish Church, and the old timber framed houses reminiscent of Tudor days just round the corner, and Monoux's Almshouses and Grammar School hard by, it is still possible to revive some of the atmosphere of the place in days long before the town we know was thought of. These treasured reminders of the earlier centuries remain, and we must prize this little area and guard it against all mischance in the future."

G.E. ROEBUCK, 1934
*(Former Borough Librarian and Hon. Secretary
of the Walthamstow Antiquarian Society.)*

The late Mr. Roebuck's words are still true today and with this revised publication the Walthamstow Historical Society hopes to spread knowledge of the Village more widely. The Village was designated a Conservation Area by the Borough Council in December 1967 and was landscaped.

The village in 2006 reflects the Local Authority's continuing interest in caring for this unique area of the Borough. When in 1934 the late George Roebuck urged that the area should be prized and cared for, no legislation existed to ensure that this happened. Today, originating from the pioneer work of William Morris in founding the Society for the Protection of Ancient Buildings in 1877, legislation does exist to enable 'Conservation Areas' to be established and maintained in our villages, towns and cities.

Walthamstow village is however just one of several conservation areas designated in Waltham Forest. Others have been established to preserve the more visually attractive aspects of the predominantly Victorian growth of the Borough. Whilst these may lack the historical interest of the Walthamstow village area they nevertheless help to remind residents that our towns can still be pleasant places in which to live; a sentiment again that William Morris continually expressed in his lectures and writings. If he returned to the 'village' today perhaps he would withdraw his remark that he was born in Walthamstow: "once a pleasant place enough, but now terribly cocknified and choked up by the jerry-builder".

J.W. HOWES, F.L.A.
*(Former Borough Librarian and a
Vice-President of the Walthamstow Historical Society.)*

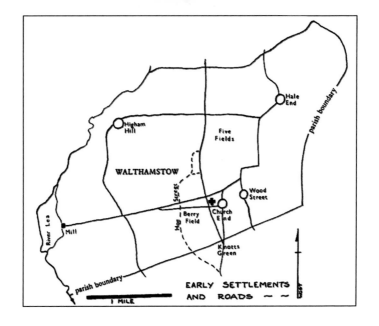

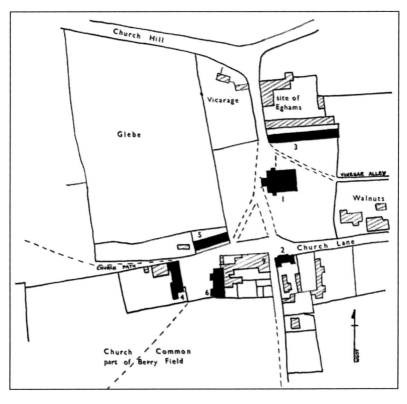

*The village of Church End as shown on John Coe's 1822
map of Walthamstow. The figures correspond to those in the text.*

Setting the Scene - the Early Settlements and Roads.

Evidence for the early story of Walthamstow is so scanty that the following account up to the 17th century is largely conjectural but it represents the most likely course of events, after considering the clues, both documentary and 'on the ground'. Probably in the mid-seventh century about 75 people (based on the hides mentioned in Domesday)[1] settled in four clearings in the forest which covered the area now known as Walthamstow. These four sites were at Higham Hill, Hale End, Wood Street and on Church Hill. The clearings are now represented by the areas round Sutton Road, The Lord Brooke (formerly the Royal Oak) between Vallentin and Havant Roads, and the Church Lane/Shernhall Street junction. A fifth village settlement Chapel End arose at a much later time, at the beginning of the 14th century, under the aegis of Salisbury Hall manor house. Tracks joined the settlements and are marked today by Billet Road and Wadham Road, and by Hale End Road and the east end of Forest Road (formerly Hagger Lane). Wyatt's Lane, Prospect Hill, Church Hill, High Street (formerly Marsh Street) and Copper-mill Lane formed the route from the Hale End and Wood Street settlements to the marshes and the watermill on the River Lea used for grinding corn (Saxon mills were water-powered, the windmill not being introduced in England until about 1190). If this assumption be correct, then it follows that Blackhorse Lane and Blackhorse Road was the route from Higham Hill to the mill and Markhouse Road was the route from Mark House and Leyton, later acting as the way to London from the lower end of Walthamstow. Another route which may well be of early origin is that of Church Lane, Church End, Church Path, St. Mary Road, Selborne Road and Willow Walk. This would be a more direct route to the watermill from the Church Hill settlement.

[1] A hide was an area of about 120 acres.

In this early period, Knott's Green, on the border with Leyton, seems to have been the junction of two routes going north across Walthamstow. One is represented by the path linking Grove Road with Shernhall Street and on to Wyatt's Lane and the other (which seems to be the oldest route of all) is represented by the line of Beulah Path, Orford Road, St. Mary's Churchyard, The Drive, Hurst Road, then across the Town Hall grounds to the road to Chingford and beyond. It is possible that this route over the hill was unsuitable for wheeled traffic and so the lower route from Leyton Green along Hoe Street via Bell Corner to the foot of Hurst Road became the more important in later centuries, leaving Church End undisturbed by the increase in traffic.

Forest Road is a later mediaeval track forming a cross-link between the north-south routes which had been in existence for several centuries and no doubt the forest had been cleared across its line long before it came into use. One huge early clearing seems to have taken place in what is now the Town Hall/College/Monoux School area where there were five great fields. Their sites can be traced from documents and the whole area lies bounded by Forest Road, Hale End Road, Wadham Road and Chingford Road. Another large clearing in the forest was Berry Field, part of which was later known as Church Common. The original Berry Field may have extended as far as Hoe Street in the west and Church Hill in the north. As it was gradually enclosed the new fields were given other names.

Although settlements and tracks developed Walthamstow was not an entity until a parish church was built. When this was placed where St. Mary's stands today it made Church End the most important of the settlements and the "centre" of Walthamstow. Church End is the only one of the original settlements still recognisable as a village nucleus and it is this heritage of the past, this special grouping of buildings, that has been declared a Conservation Area.

Church End - Its Development (Figures refer to the end maps)

A reconstruction of the development of Church End must start with a small collection of dwellings at the junction of Church Lane and Shernhall Street where probably started the "muddy stream" which gave Shernhall Street its name. Situated on the south-east side of the hill, overlooking the Wood Street valley, the village would benefit from the morning and afternoon sun whilst being protected by the brow of the hill (rising another thirty to forty feet) from the prevailing westerly winds. Round each dwelling was its individual close of land, whilst there were larger communal fields for the growing of grain in alternate years. One field probably lay between Shernhall Street and the line of Orford Road, and the other (the original Berry Field) between there and Hoe Street, both extending north to Church Hill. In a second stage forest clearance was continued over the brow of the hill northwards towards the present Forest Road and then later to the five great fields already mentioned.

The siting of the church [1] with its west door abutting on the old north-south route across the hill raised the status of the settlement. The manor house was built at the junction of the two original fields alongside the same road (where the Ancient House [2] is now) and later the village inn (Nag's Head [10]) was sited opposite. After the Norman Conquest the church was given to Holy Trinity Priory, Aldgate, together with a gift of land which seems to have embraced the whole of the great field to the north, although the part to the west of Aubrey Road was lost at an early date. Other lands in various parts of Walthamstow were added later as pious benefactions. A house for a priest would have been provided by the early part of the 13th century, probably on the site of the vicarage which was taken over by the High School in 1974 Clear proof of such siting dates from the 15th century. The present vicarage was built at the rear of the Monoux Almshouses on Temple's Fields - once the area grazed by the the dairy herd belonging to Temple's Farm.

Other buildings clustered round the churchyard: on the north side a farmhouse called Eghams and in the 16th century the Monoux Almshouses [3]. On the east side stood the Walnuts, whilst to the south some cottages were built adjoining the Nag's Head. Berry Field was gradually subdivided and in 1729 a further enclosure was taken out for the building of a workhouse [4]. In 1795 came the Squires' Almshouses [5] followed by the other cottages on Church Path. The National School [6] was built at the eastern end of the workhouse acre in 1819 and adjoining was a small coach-house which later housed the parish fire-engine. Five years later the infants' school was founded in a barn belonging to the Vicar, having its own building [7] erected on a corner of the Vicar's glebe in 1828.

After the enclosure of Church Common in 1850 the centre of activity moved from the old village nucleus to the Orford Road area and the adjacent Beulah, Eden and Summit Roads. Here were built a new Nag's Head [10] in 1859, a school in 1866, the new houses of the 1870's and the cottages for the working men. Here also was established the Town Hall in 1876, a shopping area, the hospital (1894) and the Church House and Hall (1911-14). Meanwhile a barrier between the old and new nuclei had been dug by the coming of the Great Eastern Railway in 1869/70. The Orford Road area was the "centre of the town" until the new Town Hall was opened in Forest Road in 1941. The commercial centre had already moved to the Church Hill/High Street/Hoe Street crossing and the old village was left in peace. Since then the Connaught Hospital and Church Hall have been demolished and the sites developed for housing .

In 1979-80 the Village underwent a considerable alteration. The roadway was narrowed and made one way (westwards), trees were planted and new street lighting installed.

(1) ST. MARY'S CHURCH - the ancient parish church of Walthamstow.

W.G.S. Tonkin

The church is first mentioned in an undated document by which Alice de Toni granted it to Holy Trinity Priory, Aldgate, London. Dr. P. H. Reaney assigns it to approximately 1145. Tradition credits Ralph de Toni (d.1126) with the rebuilding of the church and it is probable that a wooden one had already existed by the end of the Saxon times. The choice of site was undoubtedly influenced by the presence of the early cross roads (the junction of Orford Road with Church Lane) and as the church was built with its west door fronting on to the old north-south road.

The original building was probably rectangular, 48 feet long by 26 feet wide (this being the area now enclosed by the pillars of the nave), with a small apsidal sanctuary at the east end, and after rebuilding it would have been composed of flint rubble. If it followed the normal development a north aisle would have been built during the 13th century, south aisle in the 14th and a tower and extended chancel in the 15th century. The north aisle was certainly built of flint and the tower of Kentish ragstone; but there must have been something seriously wrong with the workmanship of the latter as it was constantly in need of repair. Indeed from 1517 it seems to have been assumed that the tower would need rebuilding.

From the various mediaeval wills it is possible to gain some idea of the internal appearance of the church prior to the Reformation. It is clear that there was a statue of St. Mary on the north side of the altar, that there was a screen and rood-loft and that somewhere within the church was a statue of St. Catherine.

A great deal of work was carried out in the year 1535. George Monoux repaired the north aisle (the trouble seems to have been mainly with the roof) and built a chapel at the east end of it. This chapel is out of line with the rest of the church. He also successfully dealt with the tower - work which entailed the demolition of the upper two-thirds and its rebuilding with brick. On the inner (or eastern) side of the tower demolition had to be carried even lower to within seven feet of the ground, which obviously necessitated the removal of part of the church roof. At the same time the south aisle was completely demolished and rebuilt, with a new chapel being built at its eastern end, and a south porch added. Both the chapels were fitted with rectangular east windows and it is known that the one on the south side contained the figures of the four Evangelists.

During all this time the church had been the property of the Holy Trinity Priory at Aldgate and some - if not all - of the Vicars during this period had been monks from there. The Priory was dissolved in 1531 and for a time King Henry VIII retained the Walthamstow properties in his own possession. He actually appointed four of the Vicars to the living and may thus technically be classed as Rector of Walthamstow.

The next important changes in the fabric of the church came in the 18th century. The population was increasing steadily and more accommodation was required. In 1710 a gallery was built at the west end of the church followed by one on the south side in 1774 and on the north side in 1807. The side galleries extended out to the pillars;

but they were not carried over the chapels, extending eastwards only as far as the chancel arch. The chapels were not, however, used for their original purposes - in fact a corner of the Monoux Chapel was screened off and used as a robing room.

Between 1817 and 1819 the east end of the church underwent considerable change. The old windows were bricked up, the walls heightened, the present windows cut and the galleries were carried right through to the east end. In 1830 a vestry room was built on the outside with a doorway through to the church on the north side of the altar. Thirteen years later the rest of the church was made uniform by raising the height of the walls, filling in the old windows and cutting new ones. In 1876 the galleries were "thrown back" from the pillars and the plaster ceiling of the nave removed.

In 1936 the east wall was found to be cracking and the opportunity was taken of making an extension of the chancel and putting in choir stalls - until that time the choir had been accommodated in the west gallery. At the same time the new east window was inserted and the vestries built on either side of the chancel extension. This work was completed in 1938. During World War II - in October 1940 - six incendiary bombs destroyed the roof of the south aisle and the gallery on that side was demolished to provide the necessary timber for repair.

The most notable monuments in the church are those of Lady Lucy Stanley (1601), which may possibly be the work of William Cure; Dame Mary Merry (1633) which is by Nicholas Stone; and the Trafford monument showing Sigismund Trafford (d.1723) as a Roman senator and his wife Susannah (d.1689) dressed as a Roman matron.

There are four brasses in the church - Henry Crane, Vicar (1436) and William Rowe (1596), both inscriptions only. George Monoux (1544) and the (palimpsest) brass of Thomas Hale (1588). The Monoux brass was reset to mark the 75th anniversary of the

Walthamstow Historical Society in honour of Peter Hogg, a member and office bearer for many years and a Vice-President.

The various furnishings of the church are dated as follows: pulpit carved oak, 1903; lectern brass, 1903; altar - oak, 1904; reredos - carved oak in high relief, a copy of Leonardo da Vinci's "Last Supper", 1905; font - white marble, 1714; royal arms - wood, painted and gilded, 1742 (restored 1953). The church was re-seated in oak between 1924 and 1932 - the style of pews was said to be based on those of St. Martin-in-the-Fields.

The churchyard contains about three and one third acres of which the older part forms an irregular rectangle round the church. An extension on the north-east side was added in 1850. There are about 1,300 visible monuments, although the whole area contains about 26,000 burials. Four of the tombs, including two table tombs, are listed buildings.

(2) THE ANCIENT HOUSE - a 15th century "hall" house.

This stands on the corner of Orford Road and Church Lane. It is a 15th century timber-framed building composed of central hall with wings originally filled in with wattle and daub. The building was restored in 1934 (when the wattle and daub was replaced by small red brick) in memory of William George Fuller by his wife and children - the work being carried out by E. Fuller & Sons, a well known local firm of building contractors.

It is believed that the house stands on the site of the former manor house of Walthamstow and was built after the "new" manor house - originally called Toni Hall - was erected in Shernhall Street. The Ancient House may be the building referred to by Sir William Hyll (Vicar of Walthamstow 1470 - 87) in his will: "a tenement of myne called John Kykylwoldys . . . and ij acres [2 acres] in buryfield buttying on the same tenement". The external chimney is 16th century.

The first clear reference to the house is in 1668. It was copyhold of Walthamstow Toni manor and at this time the copyholder was John Ash of Hackney. Besides the house the property included 12 acres in Berry Field, 14½ acres to the south of the house extending as far as the present Addison Road, comprising Sandpit and Middle Fields, 21 acres in the Marshes and Great and Little Teggs Fields - 10 acres, now represented by Church Hill Road and the properties on the south side of Prospect Hill.

John Ash died in 1689 and was succeeded by his son John who held it until his death in 1722. In 1711 he had, however, disposed of the Berry Field holdings. John Ash did not live at the house and the tenant during the later 1690's was William Grimes, who spent his last years in the Monoux Almshouses, where he died in 1708. John Ash had four daughters and the property was divided between them.

Mary died in 1728 and Elizabeth in 1736. Sarah and Anne were both married - Sarah to Osborn Skinner, a Fishmonger of London, and Anne to Theophilus Green, Apothecary of Chelmsford. Anne died in 1744 leaving a daughter also named Anne. Sarah died about 1748 and her husband less than two years later. Osborn Skinner's brother William, living at Ledbury in Herefordshire, inherited Sarah's share and sold it to Theophilus Green in 1757. His daughter having died five years before, Theophilus was now the sole copyholder.

At this date the house was described as having been "formerly called White House", situated and being near the church stile, and divided into two tenements. The insertion of the upper floor and dormer windows in the central part of the house would have taken place by this date. Theophilus Green dismembered the property selling the 14 acres behind the house to John Pistor, the land in the Marshes to Thomas Fletcher, Teggs Field to Catherine Allen and the house itself to Richard Cooke, a Victualler of Walthamstow who may well have been a landlord of the Nag's Head. Cooke's family held the house until 1811, when Charles Cooke, the copyholder, had recently died leaving his brother George as heir. But "George Cooke went abroad many years ago and is now presumed to be dead", so the property passed to his surviving daughter, Mary Elizabeth, wife of William Smith.

Mary Smith immediately sold the house to Elizabeth Lucking, widow, for £650. Elizabeth held the property for the next forty years during which time she married John Humphreys of Clapton. It was during her ownership that the house was divided into four tenements and developed into shops. On the land still remaining round the house were built the four adjoining houses in Orford Road and the one next door in Church Lane.

The Ancient House was enfranchised (freed from manorial control and obligations) on the 1st October, 1851 for the sum of £307.16s.4d., and there the record of it in the court rolls comes to an end. In 1877 part of the building was occupied by J. Coakham, a greengrocer, and the part nearer Orford Road by I. Routledge, a draper. This continued during part of the 1880's, although by 1887 the greengrocer's had become a cobbler's shop and so continued until 1893, when it was occupied for one year by Stevens the florist.

In the 1890's the division into four separate shops became complete, but after 1908 the other enterprises were dropped and the family of Charles and Elizabeth Aley ran tea rooms and a cycle shop in the whole building. After the Great War the house saw many further changes of use in its four shops; but in 1969 - 70 the east end was converted into a private dwelling and in 1971 - 72 the remainder of the ground floor was similarly converted.

The Royal Commission on Historical Monuments, when compiling their inventory about 1914, attributed the house to the 17th century but in 1934, as a memorial to W.G. Fuller his widow and children undertook the repair and restoration of this fine house, keeping the ground floor as shops, and it was then that the crown-post roof and other evidence of its earlier date was discovered.

At the end of the 20th century a major restoration and repairs were undertaken at the Ancient House. Some of the 1934 restoration works proved to be inappropriate. In 1934 the wattle and daub was removed and replaced by small red brick. This was creating dampness in the timber frame. The most recent renovation work has exposed most of the timber frame. As with most historic timber framing the building was originally constructed using fast grown green oak with some elm. [Fast-grown oak - oak that grows straight up as it struggles for the light. It is lighter, straighter, without knots and easier to split into planks. Fast-growing oak occurs only in primary forests, for example in the countries round the Baltic area. English oak is slow-growing - there is no need for it to fight for the light.] Using dendrochronology on small samples of timber it has been possible to estimate the felling date of some of the timber in the West wing as in the range of 1564-1592. The most significant alteration to the appearance of the West wing is the creation of an oriel window and the rebuilding of the curved braces to the front and rear gables. Evidence was revealed that oriel windows that had been in the building were probably removed in the 18th century.

The West wing was converted into a two-bedroomed house. The East wing has remained untouched during the restoration and repairs. It retained its 18th century weather boarding which helped to preserve the frame. The Ancient House still continues to surprise and delight visitors to the old village.

To protect the house Orford Road has been restricted to one-way traffic and the pavement widened.

(3) MONOUX ALMSHOUSES - 16th Century.

It was on Trinity Sunday, 16th June, 1527, that Richard Vaughan, gentleman, on behalf of Nicholas Hancock, Prior of Holy Trinity, and with the consent of Thomas Hickman, Vicar of Walthamstow, "yn all theire names and stede" entered peaceably into a certain parcel of land on the north part of the churchyard. After having taken peaceable possession he then and there delivered over the same to the right worshipful master George Monoux, Alderman of London. The land is described as measuring on the north side "one hundred four score and twelve foot of Assise" and in breadth at the east end forty feet and in the middle and at the west end thirty-four feet.

The purpose of this acquisition was for Monoux to build on the land "houses for pore folkes and the edification and building for a Scole master and a ffree scole". It is not known when this was carried out but one imagines that it was done soon afterwards. The fact that possession was granted by the Prior and with consent of the Vicar shows that the land was part of the churchyard originally.

George Monoux built thirteen almshouses, the design of each being a single room. In the centre was a four-roomed house on two floors for the alms-priest schoolmaster and parish clerk living together. Two large rooms on the first floor were constructed on either side of the central house, that on the west side for a schoolroom and that on the east as a feast hall. The schoolroom had a separate staircase in a small gabled projection eight feet square sited immediately to the left of the present main entrance. This staircase was removed by about 1800. Access to the feast hall was originally by an outside wooden stair at the rear of the building and by this means the food for the feast - cooked in Eghams, the farmhouse to the north of the almshouses - was carried up into the feast hall.

Under the Monoux benefaction the alms-priest-schoolmaster was paid £6.13s.4d. a year (£6.67p), the parish clerk, who was already receiving payments from other sources, £1.6s.8d. a year (£1.33p) and each of the almsfolk received £1.10s.5d. a year (£1.52p).

Monoux appointed six trustees of his charity one of whom was the Richard Vaughan mentioned above. After Monoux's death in 1544 Vaughan decided to live at Eghams and to convert the almshouses into stables for his own use. To this end he demolished some "shades for the poor to walk under" that formerly existed at the rear of the building and also the outside stairway to the feast-hall. The indignant parishioners stopped him before he had gone too far; but the charity was considerably abused. The trustees took bribes from people wanting almshouses, kept houses empty so that they could retain the 1d. per day payable to the inhabitants, carried out little in the way of repairs and pocketed the rising profits from the charity lands.

By the 1580's the feast hall was no longer fit for the purposes that Monoux had planned and since that time has been put to other uses. Various attempts were made in the 17th century to transfer the charity to other trustees, but little seems to have come of it. A suspected encroachment by the farmer on the north side of the almshouses was proved during excavations carried out in 1953. In 1782 Walthamstow parish took over the Monoux charities and reduced the required payment from the estates in the City from £42 per annum to £21. The extra was supposed to have been made up each year from the rates but in fact this was never honoured. The almshouses were put into a better state of repair - it seems probable that the building was re-fronted at this time.

The Monoux school was closed in 1880 re-opening in the Trinity Schoolroom, West Avenue, in January, 1886. Since that time the old schoolroom has been used for many purposes. The High School used it as a classroom in the late 1950's as did the oldest children from St. Mary's Infants' School between 1966 and 1974. Today it serves as the Meeting Room and Office of the Almshouse Trustees.

On 8th October, 1940, a high explosive bomb destroyed much of the west end of the building and it remained derelict for many years before being rebuilt in 1955. The old schoolroom was reconstructed and the cut brick of the chimney on the outside of the west wall was reproduced in cement. The rebuilt part is slightly higher than the rest of the building as modern legislation demands features not formerly considered necessary in building practice.

© *Walthamstow Almshouse and General Charities.*

The Almshouses were subject to considerable improvement in the late 1990's with sympathetically designed two-storey rear extensions to provide each flat with a separate bedroom and living room.

WALTHAMSTOW.

Particulars, Plan & Conditions of Sale

OF THE VALUABLE

RESIDENTIAL & BUILDING ESTATE

COMPRISING THE COMFORTABLE

Family Residence

KNOWN AS

The "Chestnuts,"

CHURCH END.

With Charming and Well-timbered **Pleasure Grounds, Kitchen Garden and Paddock, Stabling and Coach-house.** In all about

$2\frac{1}{2}$ acres.

AND POSSESSING IMPORTANT

Frontages of 540 feet

TO

CHURCH LANE and SUMMIT ROAD.

The greater portion of the Property is Copyhold of the Manor of Walthamstow Toney and High Hall, the portion fronting Summit Road is Freehold.

The Whole will be Sold by Auction by

MR.

WM. HOUGHTON,

At the MART, TOKENHOUSE YARD, LONDON, E.C.,

On MONDAY, MAY 15th, 1911,

At TWO o'clock precisely in One Lot. WITH POSSESSION.

Particulars, Plan and Conditions of Sale may be obtained of Messrs. G. Houghton & Sons, Solicitors, 68, Finsbury Pavement, E.C., and Bridge Chambers, Hoe Street, Walthamstow, and of the Auctioneer,

58, OLD BROAD STREET, LONDON, E.C.

Telephone No. 157 London Wall.

PLAN OF
"THE CHESTNUTS"
CHURCH LANE,
WALTHAMSTOW.

FOR SALE BY AUCTION BY
Mr Wm HOUGHTON,
·1911·

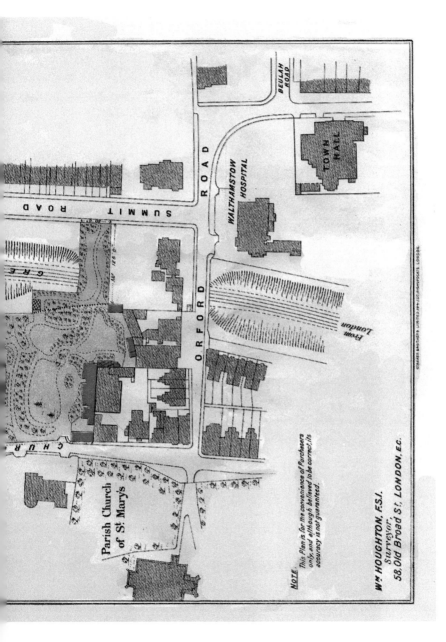

ROAD
BEULAH ROAD
TOWN HALL
WALTHAMSTOW HOSPITAL
SUMMIT ROAD
CRE
No. 126
ORFORD ROAD
CHUR
From London
Parish Church of St. Mary's

NOTE. This Plan is for the convenience of Purchasers only, and although believed to be correct, its accuracy is not guaranteed.

WM HOUGHTON, F.S.I.
Surveyor,
58, Old Broad St, LONDON, E.C.

SERAGEI BROTHERS LIMITED MFG CO. LITHOGRAPHERS. LONDON.

21

The Chestnuts, Church Lane. Drawn by Guy Osborne.

(4) VESTRY HOUSE - 18th Century.

In 1729 the Walthamstow Vestry (the local government of the time, composed of "all ratepayers in Vestry assembled") bought one acre of the Church Common for £6 and on this was built the first part of the Vestry House in 1730. As originally constructed it was an eight-roomed house on two floors with a central doorway and entrance hall. The two rooms to the right of the doorway were the front and back kitchens. On the left the room at the front was to be used by the Vestry for its meetings whilst that at the rear seems to have been the room used by the Master of the Workhouse. Upstairs were four bedrooms.

The workhouse contained some 20 - 30 poor people and not being sufficiently large was extended by a separate building being erected on the north side in 1756. This was connected to the main house by a covered way and is now represented by the Panelled Room and Loft. In 1779 the Vestry Room was enlarged by being projected forward across the courtyard and this also provided extra space upstairs. The Vestry Room was given its own exterior doorway and had a small entrance hall from which access to the Room was gained via a green baize door.

The space between the main building and the extension was partly filled by additional building in 1814 and finally closed later in the century. In 1840 the paupers were moved out to Stratford and the main house was used for Vestry purposes whilst the extension became Walthamstow's police station until 1870. The extension then served as the armoury for the local volunteers until 1891 when it became a builder's yard until 1933.

Meanwhile the original building continued to serve as a "town hall". The Vestry gave up its secular powers to the newly-formed Local Board in 1873 and both bodies continued using the house for the next three years. The Local Board, however, purchased the Public Hall in Orford Road and adapted it for use as a Town Hall, moving there in 1876. The Vestry continued to use Vestry House for about five years more and then rented rooms at the Town Hall as required.

A sketch by Walter E. Spradbery, 1947. © Vestry House Museum.

Vestry House then became the headquarters of the Walthamstow Literary and Scientific Institute, which met there for ten years from 1882 - 1892, after which it became a private dwelling house being inhabited by the Maynard family until 1912 and by Miss Constance Demain-Saunders, J. P. until 1930, when she presented the remainder of her lease to the Walthamstow Borough Council. The Council decided to use the building for the establishment of a Local Museum which was opened in May, 1931. Two years later the old extension was acquired and added to the Museum and the former exercise yard was roofed over to provide yet another room. For the first twelve months the Museum had no professional staff. It was run by a rota of volunteers from the Walthamstow Antiquarian Society (now Walthamstow Historical Society) and was only open in the evenings. Its collections were mainly two-dimensional such as maps, documents and illustrations that had been transferred from the

Borough's library collection. Gradually the number of three-dimensional objects grew. The Walthamstow Historical Society still gives financial support for the acquisition of artifacts.

The house had originally possessed a large garden which was used in the workhouse period for the growing of vegetables to supplement the diet. After closing as a workhouse seven cottages were built on the north and north western sides of the garden (four demolished in 1967). With the building of the Chingford branch railway between 1866 - 70 a triangular slice was cut off the south side and this was replaced by another triangle of land on the west.

In 1981-2 the remaining three cottages were completely re-designed internally as a Museum extension. The workhouse garden restoration was funded by the Heritage Lottery Fund and the Council. The garden was opened to great acclaim on 28th August 2002 by the Mayor, Councillor Fazlur Rahman, and John Trott, the restorer and driver of the Bremer car, and some 200 guests. The Bremer car which is now installed in a frameless display unit was built in Walthamstow by Federick William Bremer and is claimed to be the first British four-wheeled motor car with an internal combustion engine. As part of the project a community room was built providing facilities for lectures. The community room is connected to the main museum by a covered walkway. At the same time a small sunken performance area was created. Alongside the walkway is a new permanent display about the workhouse garden. Volunteers help to maintain the garden.

(5) SQUIRES' ALMSHOUSES - 18th Century.

These were founded in 1795 by Mrs. Mary Squires, a widow living at Walworth, in Surrey (according to her will proved in 1797). They were built on a narrow neck of land at the end of Short Field protruding up to the edge of the churchyard between the Church Common and the Vicar's glebeland. The almshouses were designed to accommodate six widows of Walthamstow tradesmen, of fifty years of age and upwards, or younger if they suffered from affected eye-sight or were lame. Each almswoman received £5 per year during Mrs. Squires' lifetime and after her death in 1796 had a further £8 per year added to the income. Each widow, on her entrance to an almshouse, was provided with a bedstead, a stove and a large water-tub.

The inscription above the almshouses reads: "These houses are erected and endowed for ever by Mrs. Mary Squires, widow, for the use of six decayed tradesmen's widows of this parish and no other Ano Domi 1795". It should be understood that the "decayed" refers to the widows and is used in the sense of "declined in wealth".

Under the Rules and Orders laid down by the foundress the widows were allowed to take in not more than one nurse-child, they could undertake small washing and clear-starching but not heavy washing and were not allowed to hang any article out in the front of their houses.

Late in the 20th Century the original six almshouses were reduced to four to provide modern bathrooms and kitchens for each 'widow'. This was skilfully achieved so as not to change the appearance of the original front elevation of the almshouses.

(6) NATIONAL SCHOOL -1819.

This school, in Vestry Road, was founded in 1819 to house the overflow of girls from the Monoux school which at that time was rather crowded with about forty children. Before the building was finished, however, a new policy was adopted whereby it was to become an independent school in its own right on the plan of the National Society, formed in 1811. The building was designed to accommodate 100 boys and 100 girls and also included living accommodation for the master and mistress. It was built on the easternmost part of the workhouse acre and between it and the workhouse ran the path which is now Vestry Road.

The cost of the building was met by voluntary contributions (payment of one guinea constituted a Governor). Pupils were charged 1d. per week, payable in advance, and school hours were 9 a.m. - 12 noon, 2 p.m. - 4 p.m. except Saturdays. The building was also used for the Sunday School (giving secular education to children unable to attend school during the week) which met on Sundays at 9.30 a.m. and 2 p.m. - members being expected to attend both sessions.

The school was enlarged in 1825 and in 1866 a new school for boys was built in Orford Road (this building is now the Asian Centre). In 1904 the boys and girls exchanged buildings and in 1906 the boys were transferred to the new school in Warwick (now Barret) Road.

The Vestry Road building continued to be used as a Sunday School and as Parish Rooms until 1920. It was then sold to the Senior Scouts' Association and used as an Institute until 1928 when the Scouts in turn sold it to the National Spiritualist Church.

(7) OLD FIRE STATION

Fire-engine house, next to the old National School, sketched by Annie R. Hatley, 1953.

The Parish hand-drawn fire engine was housed in the small building next to the National School (now the Spiritualist Church) and was in use for most of the 19th century. The fire engine was adapted for horse-drawn use in 1863. By 1883 the local board authorised the engine keeper to enlist six firemen, who were paid for attendance at fires providing they arrived within half an hour of a fire starting. After a new fire station in St James' Street was opened in 1887 the building was, for a long time, part of Welch's garage which moved to Erskine Road in 1977. The building is now in private use.

(8) ST. MARY'S INFANTS' SCHOOL -1828.

Samuel Wilderspin, in his book "Early Discipline Illustrated", recalls how the Infants' School came to be founded: "The Vicar of Walthamstow had, as yet, remained indifferent: repeatedly asked by his brother to visit our school, he had as frequently refused: but, at length, on inspecting it, his objections were removed, and of the practicability and efficiency of the system he became fully convinced. This he communicated to me, and asked whether I could take a survey of his parish, to ascertain if it could be adopted; his own mind doubting, as the houses were widely scattered, if a sufficient number of children could be collected. Acceding to his request, I assured him the object he desired was quite practicable, that a barn belonging to him could be appropriate to the purpose, and that our efforts might speedily commence. I subsequently laboured for five weeks at Walthamstow, with one of my daughters, in conjunction with the master, who had been sent to our school to obtain all the information he could from me during the interval. At the end of three weeks, visitors were admitted; and almost every day of the remaining fortnight we had from twenty to fifty persons. It should be stated, to the honour of the Vicar, that he spared no expense to render the Institution complete; and, that the master might possess every advantage, a gentleman, well acquainted with the system, spent there five or six weeks. The results of these exertions were highly gratifying to the reverend gentleman, and he lost no opportunity of inviting me to his house, when our conversation turned invariably on the treatment of the young. At the close of my stay, he told me he intended to write a work on the subject, which he has since done".

This was in 1824 and the book mentioned had reached its third edition by the following year. So successful was the Infants' School that the Vicar, the Rev. William Wilson, built it a permanent home on a corner of his glebe in 1828; the very first Church of England Infants' School in the country. The building was restored in 1928. It was closed as a school in 1978 and after refurbishment became the Welcome Centre.

School hours were 9 a.m.-12 noon, 2 p.m.-5 p.m. (1 p.m.-4 p.m. in winter); 9 a.m.-12 noon on Wednesdays and Saturdays. The sessions were divided into lessons lasting a quarter of an hour with half an hour's play morning and afternoon. From 4 until 4.30 was spent in "examination in that which has been learned through the day" and then school ended with "hymns, prayers, and singing".

An example of the methods used may be seen from the following "graduations by which the infants ... are introduced to the art of arithmetic". Clapping the hands in measured time, in imitation of the masters; Counting (the children placed in classes round the room); Reading figures on the board (or impressed on pieces of tin!); Learning by ear from a monitor on the rostrum, the more simple combinations of number, addition, subtraction, multiplication, division and fractions; Examination in the combinations of number; Learning by ear the most useful tables; Examination and illustration of the tables; The acquirement of the first steps in arithmetic on the arithmetical board; Writing figures on slates; Mutual examination in the combination of number, the tables and mental arithmetic; and Practice of arithmetic on slates. Perhaps it should be added that "infants" covered children aged 2 to 7 years.

In 1830 the scholars at the infants' school were joined by three so called 'savages' who had been brought to England from Tierra del Fuego on HMS Beagle on its travels under the command of Captain Robert Fitzroy. The natives were brought to England by Captain Fitzroy to be taught Christianity and English. The Beagle having docked, Fitzroy looked for support and funding for the natives and was eventually put in touch with The National Society for Providing Education of the Poor in the Principals of the Established Church. The Secretary was Rev. Joseph Wigram, son of Sir Robert Wigram of Walthamstow who knew of the work of Rev. William Wilson. The Reverend was only too happy to help. The three Fuegians, two young men and a girl were lodged either in the school or with Mr and Mrs Jenkins, the schoolmaster at their house in Church Lane. There were about 150 children attending the school and the younger boy and the girl seem to have been popular. The older boy was about 26 and was surly and increasingly anti-social and found it difficult to mix with the younger children. Captain Fitzroy had intended the 'visitors' to stay for three years but the Beagle was recommissioned in July 1831, so after little more than a year they were taken on board to return to their islands. The people of Walthamstow gave them a generous send off. A subscription fund was set up and a large quantity of European clothing, tools and ironmongery were purchased. The Beagle sailed on 27 December 1831 and on board was a Mr Charles Darwin.

(9) No. 10 CHURCH LANE.

This house was built in 1830 on land formerly part of the Ancient House garden. As originally planned it included workshops, yards and a garden and was occupied by Anthony Storey Reed, the builder. The Reed family continued in occupation of the house until the early years of the twentieth century. In the Provisional List prepared by the Ministry of Town and Country Planning in July 1950 the house is described as follows: "Two storeys, stock brick; three sashes, those on the ground floor in rounded recesses. Central Doric porch, plain eaves, hipped slate roof. The house groups well with the other old buildings surrounding the churchyard". It is also to be noted that the internal walls of the house are timber framed with brick infilling.

(10) (11) NAG'S HEAD.

The original Nag's Head Inn stood on the south-western corner of the junction of Orford Road with Church End [10]. The building was certainly in existence by the 16th century as was shewn by the presence of Tudor bricks in the wine cellar (which still exists below ground). This inn was copyhold of Walthamstow Toni manor and the property included two acres of land in the Church Common and three acres of marsh.

Between 1769 and 1774 three houses and a shed were added to the Nag's Head probably on the west side and fronting on to Church End. The occupant of the inn in 1851 was Francis Wragg, the coach proprietor, and he eventually acquired the property which was enfranchised to him in 1858 for the sum of £402 16s.0d. By then the landlord was Horace Underwood who, in the August of the following year, applied for a transfer of the licence to a new inn which had been built on the other side of Orford Road [11]. The reason for this was "The house having become by unforeseen and unavoidable calamity unfit for the reception of travellers". It is not surprising that Wragg's coach-house and yard adjoined the new Nag's Head (which presumably he also owned) and that the two enterprises should be mutually beneficial.

When the Church Common was enclosed in 1850 the two acres belonging to the inn were consolidated into 1 acre 2 roods 12 perches immediately adjoining the south side of the property. With the transfer of the licence in 1859 the old inn and cottages were demolished and on the site was built a grocer's shop and four houses. The land to the rear was used for a time as a tea-garden; but it was much reduced in size about 1880 when a shop and four houses were built on the south side of it fronting on to the railway cutting. By this date as well the two cottages in Church End next to the grocer's shop had also been converted into shops.

In the garden behind the grocer's shop there was a grape vine and a fig tree, both of which survived the many vicissitudes of the later history of the shop until both they and the building were swept away in the demolition of the early part of the year 1959. The site remains open as a paved area.

(12) The Old Town Hall, Orford Road.

The origin of the building lies in the days when Walthamstow had no proper room in which to hold concerts and other meetings. The only available place was the Infant School room in St Mary's Churchyard. The Literary Society held some entertainments in the room but it was not entirely suitable for the town's needs. In 1866, some public-spirited gentlemen purchased a piece of land in Orford Road and built a public hall, which was run by The Walthamstow Public Hall Company, and this provided the first place of entertainment. The Company failed after 10 years and the Local Board acquired the hall, building the imposing Italianate Town Hall in 1876 on the front of the original hall, which continued to be used for social activities. The building continued as The Town Hall until 1941 when the new Town Hall in Forest Road was completed. Following that the building served as a local office for the Ministry of Food and a Welfare Centre until taken over as part of Connaught Hospital, forming the main entrance until 1977 when the Hospital closed. The Waltham Forest College occupied the building as its Arts, Fashion and Design Centre. The College vacated in 1986.To find a long term use for the building was difficult. In the early 1990's the Council approved a planning application to demolish the old public hall at the rear and for the erection of 18 self-contained residential flats. By 1996, following restoration, the Italianate building was in use as a Children's Nursery.

(13) Former St Mary's National School, Orford Road.

This school situated next to the old Town Hall was built at the same time as the original public hall in 1866. Designed by William Wittington it accommodated the young boys who were sharing with the girls at the National School in Vestry Road (now the Spiritualist Church). In 1904 the boys returned to Vestry Road and the girls occupied Orford Road until the school closed in 1949. The building became the pathology department of Connaught Hospital until 1977. On 24th November 1983 it was officially opened as the Asian Centre by the Prince and Princess of Wales.

(14) No. 5 Vestry Road.

This was the Schoolhouse, also designed by William Wittington and built at the same time as the National School in Orford Road. Originally Vestry Road forked where No.5 is now. This fork in the road ran parallel to Orford Road where Berryfield Close is, to the rear of where Connaught Hospital was later developed. The other fork went to the forecourt of Vestry House. In this section were four semi-detached houses, two each side of the road. The Great Eastern Railway purchased the houses for demolition to enable the railway cutting to be formed.

The railway cutting. Nag's Head in the background.
W.G.S. Tonkin

(15) No. 11 Orford Road.

Alfred Janson constructed this substantial and attractive mid-Victorian villa, originally called "Dunheved" after the enclosure of the Church Common in 1850, along with St Mary's Church House, which also survives on the corner of the junction of Orford and Summit Roads. The building, which is included in the local listed buildings, was at one time owned by the Health Authority as part of Connaught Hospital, the main complex of which was opposite. In the 1990's a residential care home was built in the rear garden. Care was taken that the new development was sympathetic to the surrounding area, retaining as many mature trees as possible on the site. The railway tunnel passes under the northern half of the site. The house is now divided into residential flats.

(16) Former Post Office Sorting Office, Vestry Road.

One of the Dutch gables, left, and part of the foliated freeze, below.

Walthamstow Urban District Council applied in 1899 for improvements to the postal service facilities and they were duly advised that 'arrangements are under consideration for acquiring a site for a new postman's office for sorting purposes'. It was not until 1903 that the new sorting office in Vestry Road was opened to replace the office on Hoe Street railway bridge. The sorting office building is of architectural interest with extensive terracotta in the full-length foliated frieze and its Dutch gables. The sorting office became surplus to requirements when the new sorting office was opened in Church Hill. The building is now the Sakina Trust Centre.

(17) The Chestnuts, Nos. 19-21 Bishops Close.

A Grade II listed mansion built between 1820-1836. It was the home of Rev. James Foulkes Roberts who was headmaster of the Monoux School and also ran a boarding school at the house. Originally set in extensive landscaped grounds which in 1911 included pleasure grounds and a large paddock, in all about 2½ acres. (Map centre pages.) The property in 1911 was still a copyhold of the Manor of Walthamstow Toni and High Hall except a small portion of the estate with a frontage to Summit Road, which was freehold subject to the rights of the Great Eastern Railway Company in respect of the tunnel below. Several years ago the house was converted into four flats. (Illustration on page 22.)

Walthamstow Estate Agency Offices.

KING'S

TAX   OFFICE

WALTHAMSTOW.

FRAS. J. L. KING,
COLLECTOR AND ASSESSOR
OF
INCOME TAX, HOUSE DUTY AND LAND TAX.

Estate, Land and General Insurance
Agent.

RENTS COLLECTED
& ESTATES MANAGED.

ENCL:

17, Church Hill,
(near Hoe Street Station GER.)

Walthamstow, N.E.

Friday 29th December 1911.

NAT. TEL. NO. 647 WALTHAMSTOW.

Dear Madam,

      re "The Chestnuts", Church Lane.

Herewith I beg to enclose Official receipt for your cheque of £36:15:0.

Yours truly,

Mrs A Day,

Thorpe Coombe,

Forest Road, Walthamstow.

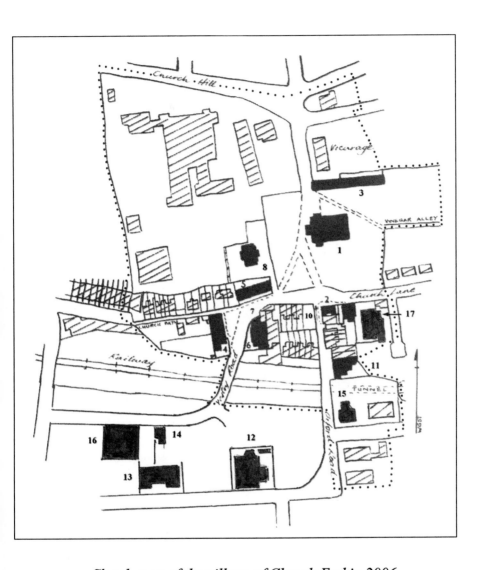

Sketch map of the village of Church End in 2006.
The numbers correspond to those in the text.
The red dotted line marks the boundary of the Walthamstow Village
Conservation Area.

References:

Walthamstow Past and Present. Gilbert Houghton 1929

"Orford Road" and *"Walthamstow Village"*.
London Borough of Waltham Forest Conservation Area Leaflets

Walthamstow Past. David Mander
Published by Historical Publications 2001.

Timber Framed Survey and Interpretation Report.
Butler & Hegarty Architects 2002

Vestiges No 51 1963, Vestry House Museum.